MAESTRA

Maestra

FLOWERSONG
PRESS

POEMS BY

ANGELINA SÁENZ

FLOWERSONG
PRESS

FlowerSong Press
Copyright © 2024 by Angelina Sáenz
ISBN: 978-1-953447-25-8

Published by FlowerSong Press
in the United States of America.
www.flowersongpress.com

Illustrations and their captions are based on the social media posts
of Angelina Sáenz.

Illustrations and Cover Art by Lorna Alkana
Cover Design by Lorna Alkana and Priscilla Celina Suarez
Set in Adobe Garamond Pro
Captions set in Andale Mono and Noto Emoji

NOTICE: SCHOOLS AND BUSINESSES
FlowerSong Press offers copies of this book at quantity discount with
bulk purchase for educational, business, or sales promotional use. For
information, please email the Publisher at info@flowersongpress.com.

I dedicate this book to all the children in public schools
and their allies

&

to the revolutionary educators
Tsunesaburo Makiguchi and Josei Toda

The purpose of education is the happiness of children.

—Tsunesaburo Makiguchi

The message of unconditional positive regard is, "I care about you.
You have value. You don't have to do anything to prove it to me, and
nothing's going to change my mind."

I sometimes try to imagine myself radiating unconditional positive
regard like a glow around me when I walk into a classroom but I also
actually say those words to my students in ways that fit our relationship.

I make sure to tell them I care about them, regardless
of what they accomplish or achieve in our academic work together.

— Alex Venet

I have never encountered any children in any group who are not geniuses.
There is no mystery on how to teach them. The first thing you do is treat
them like human beings and the second thing you do is love them.

— Asa Hilliard

Table of Contents

PARENTS

¡HUELGA!

COVID

Girl

How have 30 minutes passed and you have only done three math problems?

> (Giggling)
> I'm thinking

Do you know what you're doing?

> Yes

I'm going to ask you again
Do you know what you're doing?

> (Serious)
> I'm not sure

So, here's the deal
you are responsible
for keeping track
of when you don't know
and as soon as you feel unsure
you run to my desk to get help
Do you understand?

> Yes, Señora Sáenz

I'm putting a post-it
with your name on it

in front of me
and I am setting an alarm for five minutes
on my phone
so that I check in with you
¿Entendido?

 Si, Señora Sáenz

You are too smart and too important
to not do your work

Vocesitos

Señora Sáenz
if you see me tilting my head

it's because I'm thinking

Good morning! 🐚

Señora Sáenz
are you afraid of La Llorona?

No mijo
I'm afraid of ICE

They are the creators of La Llorona

El Principito por Antoine de Saint-Exupéry

Ezekiel Seraen

El Principito book report covers. Their work perpetually inspires me. My name is Angelina, and I teach children.

Sra. Sáenz
did you brush your hair today?

      Did you cook two breakfasts?
      Make two lunches?
      Drive one son to college?
      Help the other one get dressed
      'cause he's wearing a cast?
      And sort the dogs out before you left home?

Of course, I didn't do all that

      Well, I did
      and no, I did not brush my hair this morning

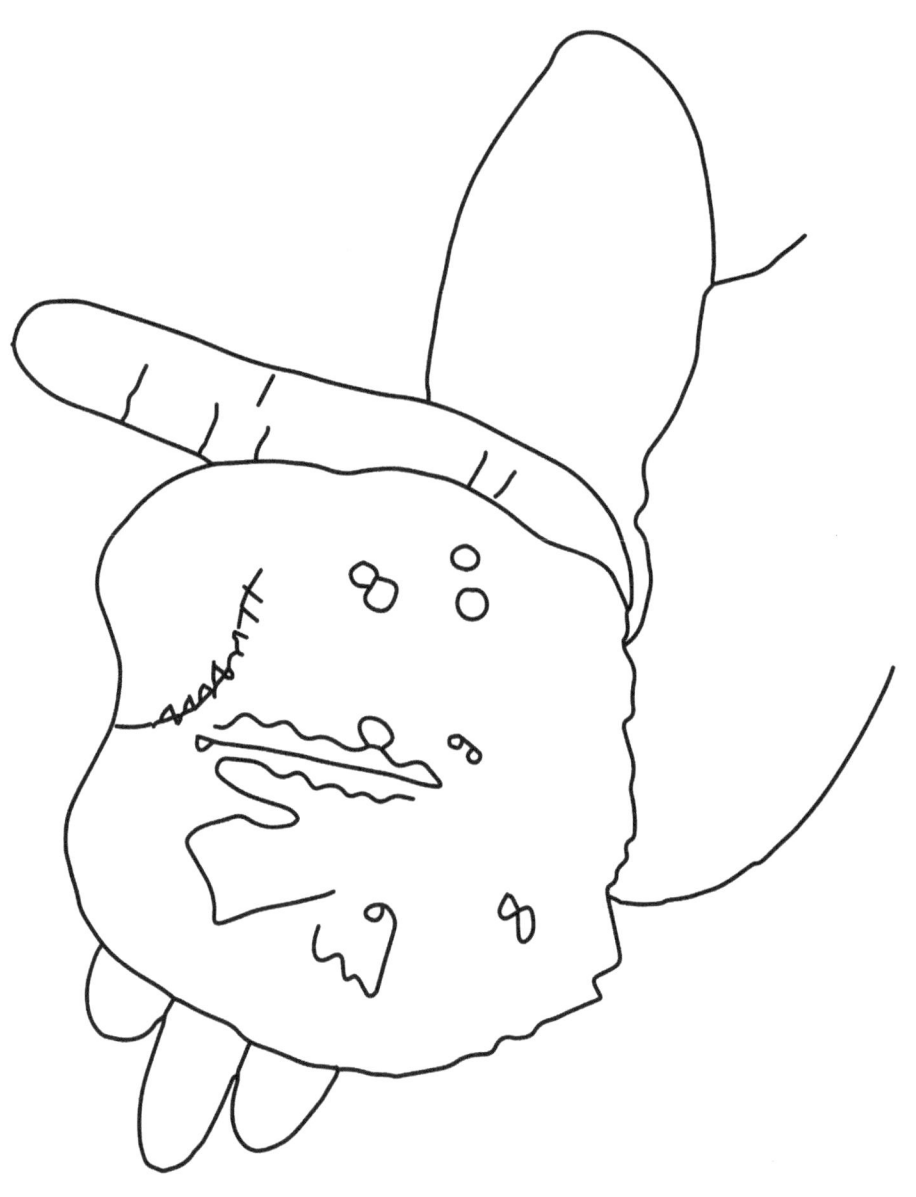

¡Senora Sáenz, te hice una pupusa de plastilina!
¿Con Queso y loroco? ¡Claro que sí!

Why are you laying your torso across the desk?

Why is your whole body on furniture in my classroom?
Are you a creature who crawls on furniture
or a boy at school, sitting properly in my class?

      I am not a creature

So, are you a person? A human who knows how to sit down?

      Señora Sáenz, I am a man

Shoe laces

Teacher says

>   Don't know how to tie shoes
>   then wear slip-ons or Velcro
>   I have too many kids to be tying shoes all day long

I tell my mom
I need slip-ons or Velcro
and she sends me to school with laces again

I walk around all day
with my shoes untied

Sometimes
I tuck them in on the side

Tell me the story you wrote

First, I went to a party
Then, they killed an animal in front of me
Last, we ate it

Tell me the story you wrote II

First, I was at home
Then, there was a ghost in my room
Last, he stayed

      You know, these are personal narratives
      You have to write about real experiences you have

Yeah, a ghost lives in my house

Thinking of all the psychics and brujxs in my life who see the dead
Okay mijo, great story

Tell me the story you wrote III

First I got an airplane
Then I landed in Switzerland
Last, I played in the snow

     I want to be in Switzerland right now

Me too

**Happy new year! Welcome back to Kindergarten!
What happened to you?**

      I broke my thumb and fractured my hand

Wow. How did that happen?

      When I was visiting my Dad in jail
      The steel door closed on my hand
      I have a note
      I can't play outside until February
      I have to go to the office at recess and lunch

Well, I'm glad to see you
Put your backpack away and come sit on the rug

      Are you going to read us a story?

Yes

      Can you please read the story about the hedgehog
      who thinks the acorn is his baby?

Of course

Today is Cat Day

Today is cat day
Today is cat day
Today is cat day

      Every day is cat day for you

Every day is cat day for everyone

cats

Cats are cule
Cats are climbers
Cats are afraid of water
7 of us have cats

Meow. 🐱

We will be studying the sky for the next few weeks

What is in the sky?

      My uncle

Your uncle is in the sky?

      Yes, he is in heaven and heaven is in the sky
      So is Jesus
      the sun
      the moon
      stars
      birds
      an eagle
      that's still a bird
      a butterfly
      clouds
      and God

9 DAYS TO GO

Single digits, bitches! ☼ (And yes, I painted that…)

Señora Sáenz, you write so fast

It's because I'm 50
I've been writing for decades

> What?
> I never want to turn 50
> Omg, you are so old
> You might almost die
> You know how old my mom is?
> Then you'll be 51
> I never knew that about you
> Wow
> I think that's how old my grandma is
> What is a decade?

Incredible first day of school! We launched Writer's Workshop and I wrote alongside my kids. Shared about the morning I arrived at Texas A&M at 7:30 am for Macondo, met a nice administrator who gave me a tour, showed me where to take a nap while I waited for the dorm room and about the cafeteria lady who gave me a chicken strip platter instead of just the fries I ordered because she wanted me to have "a good lunch." The kids loved that I wrote too. They had sincere questions. Why were you there so early? How come you couldn't get in dorm? Were you afraid to sleep in a random study room? Really going to teach them how to write and participate for the table, and how to study examples from mentor texts for their own writing. I'm actually going to study one page from Ocean Vuong and discuss it with them. ♡

**Walking down the hallway I compliment my student
on the wonderful essay he wrote about his love for his father**

I ask why he was absent
and he says because he took his father
to the border
so he can catch a flight
back to El Salvador

      Porque no tiene papeles

This student sat in front of me all day today
did his work
laughed with his friends
and carried on

but that moment
when I realized how he spent his weekend
we locked eyes
and he began to cry
and so did I

Tangrams may or may not bring children to tears. 🀄😢

Me siento mal

Hoy se opera mi mamá
y tengo que cuidar
a mi hermana de 2 años
hasta que mi mamá se alivia

Mi papá trabaja todo el día
y mis abuelos son muy viejos para ayudarme

¿Crees que puedo cuidar a mi hermanita?

Señora Sáenz
I just want to be at home

watch shows
play with my toys
wear my dragon pajamas
play a game on my phone
paint, color, play with my mom
and all that stuff

That's just where I'd rather be
I'm tired of school
I hope that doesn't hurt your feelings
It's not you

Who helped you write this?

      I wrote it myself

No, you didn't

      You don't think I know how to write
      family, *my* and *go*?

No, I don't
Class, who helped Robert write this?

      He wrote it himself

Hmmm. How do you know these words?

      I copied it off the chart and wall like you taught me

Wow, I am impressed

      and I am learning

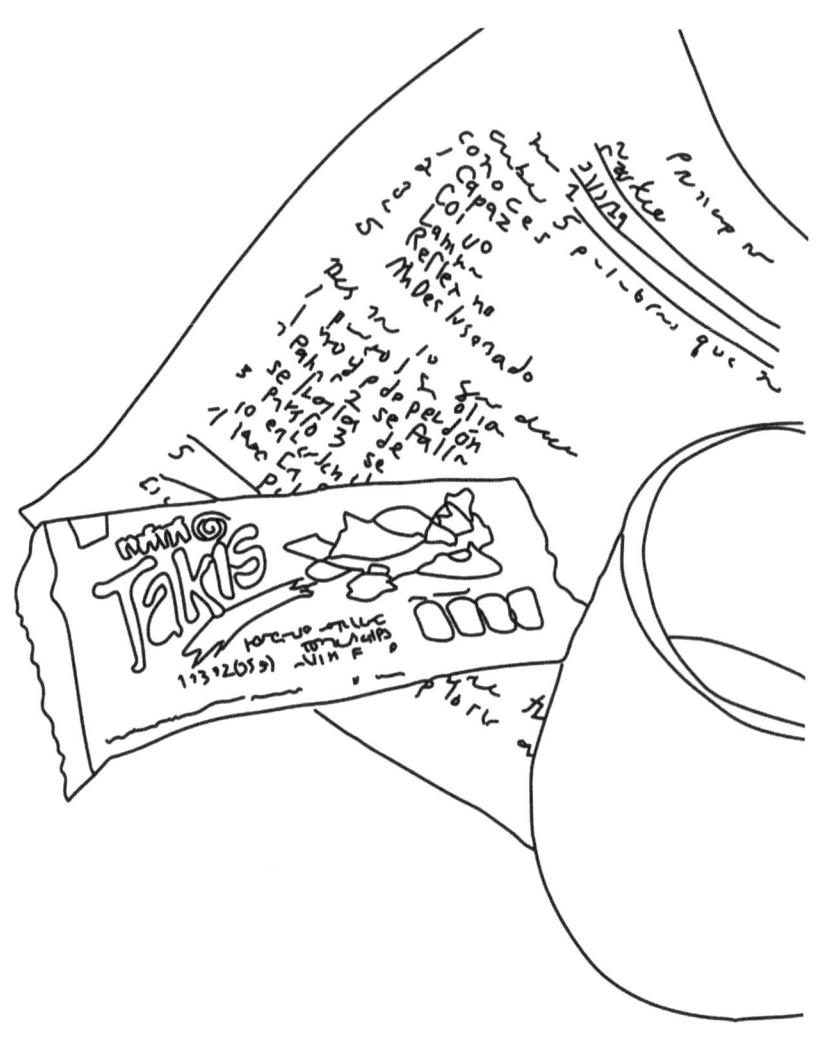

The first taki pack of the year given to me by a student!
It's official! School has started. And you KNOW I killed that shit!
✊

Señora Sáenz, do you know how to handle mosquito bites?

Well, I have A+ blood
and that is what mosquitoes and ants love

If you do not get bitten
then you have C- blood

I have good blood
but it's bad
because I get bitten all the time
I have so many other people's blood in me now

I use perfume on mosquito bites

> One, it cleans the bite
> Two, it takes away the itch
> Three, it makes you smell pretty

I should write an All About Mosquito Bites book

Señora Sáenz
I googled you

You are relevant

Profesorxs

We want teachers to

respect, support and go all out for students and families

yet we don't

respect, support or go all out for teachers

Ready or not! 🖋

My colleague is disabled
and cannot get up and down the stairs

There are things
called elevator keys
but he is told
that there is not an extra copy for him
and they don't know when facilities can provide one

So when he wants to leave his floor
he has to either meet a campus aide at the elevator
at the designated time
(if he or she misses this designated time, he is assed out)
or he has to call the office
for someone to come and open the elevator for him

One day
there was no one around to get him off the second floor
so he said he'd walk down two flights of stairs with me
I told him no, it was too dangerous
We could stay in his room and have lunch
and he started to cry

Teacher

A man
mostly women
who is educating your child
times 24-34 other children
Whose classroom is a mix of personalities, readiness levels and learning styles
Who is actually getting them to learn and apply new content
while also teaching them to be a part of the classroom community
They deal with all of the adults (colleagues, administrators, and parents)
and most of the time are social workers (and not just with the working
class students)

Please consider this
before you communicate with us

Text message from a colleague

Some mornings
as my kids slop syrup all over the place
(during breakfast in the classroom)
and I can't get online to take attendance
(because our wireless is down, AGAIN)
or we can't work on grades because the portal is fucked up
or when I am getting interrupted every two seconds
for non-instructional bullshit
and my (insert # here) kids are tripping over each other
because there is no space between desks
I wonder why I didn't enter
a civilized profession

Students will not learn from you

If you have contempt
      for them
      their families
      their language
      their community
      and their culture

I am not a person who has a lot of questions

but there are some at my school who do
and they dominate faculty meetings
with their endless fucking clarifications

No DIY up in this mug

I've asked my principal to dismiss the mofos who don't have questions
before he opens the floor to questions
but he doesn't
Lmfao
Now in the virtual world
I've been added to a faculty group chat
and as you can imagine
homeys ask endless questions on the thread
I've since left that chat
Asked my principal to not include me again
and suggested he start a chat titled

"No estén chingando"

and for all the people chingando

to go there to ask all their pinche questions

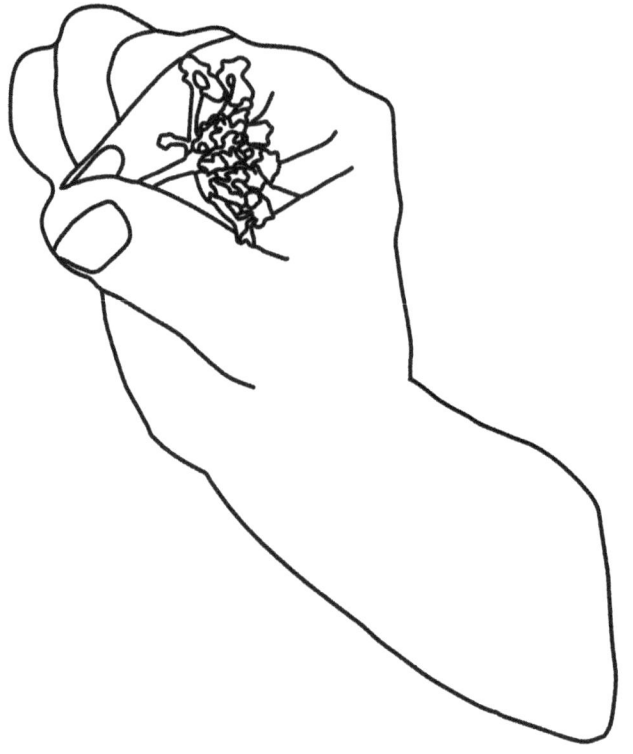

Maestra, para ti.

In the workroom, my colleague says

None of these parents care, Sáenz

      My mom didn't care, I tell her

And that's why I'm proud of you

      Yeah, but don't give up on the kids
      because their parents are struggling
      It would be like giving up on me

You do not

       deserve
       have the heart
       or the will

           to teach
           poor, students of color

You do not see
that your disrespectful and uncaring actions
are the foundation of their lifelong occupation
of hating and doubting themselves and feeling inadequate

In the hallway

Teachers talk about
how they don't cash out their coins anymore
because the machine charges nine cents on the dollar

We talk in pennies y'all

Pennies

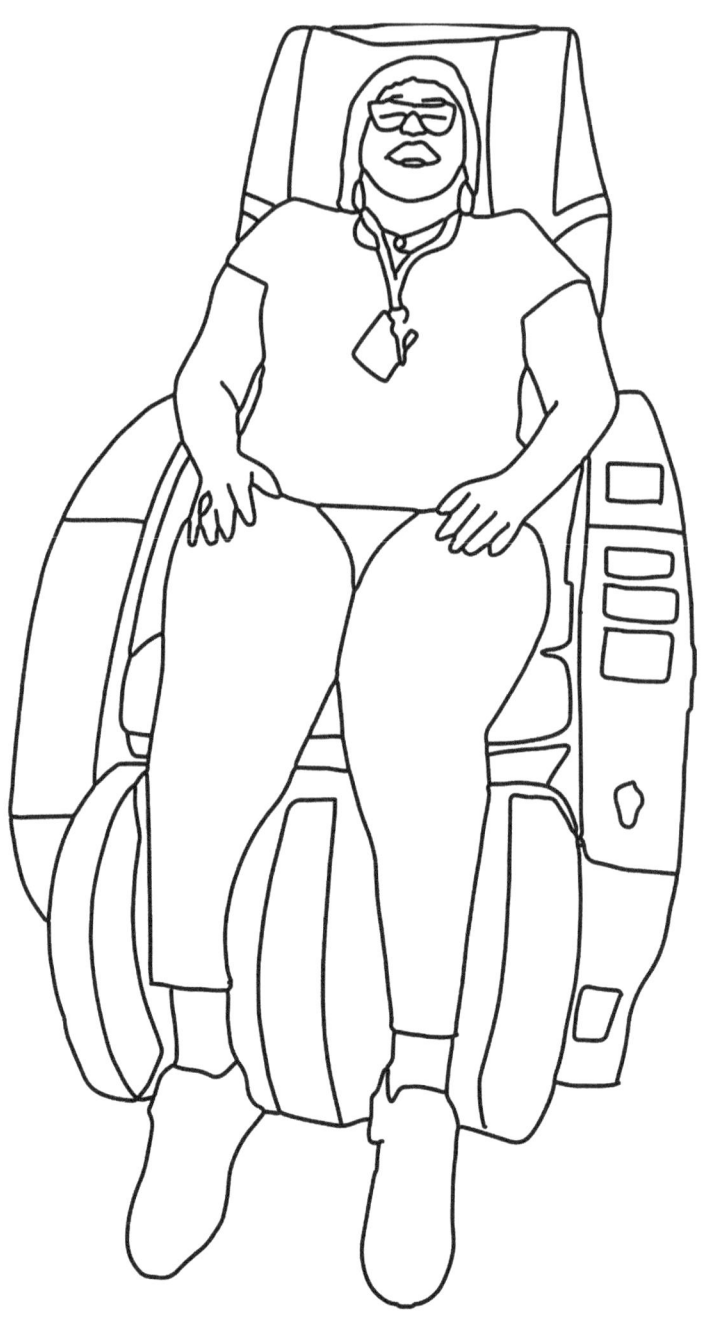

Omens! We are off to a genius start! #MassageCharinTeacherLounge
#WeShouldntHaveToPayThough

Teachers show up

to teach your children
even when
they have cancer
their children are sick
they have no gas to get to school
they're losing their home
they go home to their dying loved one
their body is aching from their chronic disease

They open their eyes
and the world is heavy on their shoulders
and they go to school
to teach your children

Parents

Hero

My kindergarten student's father
the man who found every way to talk with me
when school started
Who knew nothing about zoom, google classroom
schoology, passwords and emails
El de un pueblo montañoso de Michoacán
Who sits with his son during every virtual class
His brown finger approaching the screen
to mute and unmute his son
when he shares his work
and then takes off after our session to his swing shift 50 miles away
assured me today
that his son is learning and knows more than it appears
because his son
my kindergarten student
just translated
for his parents and doctors at Children's Hospital
where his brother was taken
after being in a car accident

One of my favorite parents, picking up her son from school
in pantuflas.🖤 #IComeFromAPlace

A mom tells me during parent conferences
that her six-year-old says he doesn't want to come to school

They are from the countryside in El Salvador
Schools there are different and the teacher had a different style

I tell her that we are crazy in this country
not letting kids play, putting all kinds of pressure on them to learn
and not respecting their developmental levels

I tell her, her son is onto something and if I were him
in this big building, with this new language,
con esta gente pesada con sus agendas pesadas
I wouldn't want to come to school either

I sent a message to a parent yesterday

> Good morning. Your child has not returned
> their book bags with two books. Please return
> it tomorrow. If it is not returned tomorrow (lost),
> you will have to pay $10 per book and your child
> will no longer take books home. Thank you.

After, I thought about if my mom would have received that message

She probably would have

1. Not read it
2. Told the teacher to fuck off
3. Kicked my ass for not having the bag
4. Made a toast with an Olde English to the asshole teacher
   and her asshole message

But she would have made NO effort
to find the bag or pay $10 per book

Sometimes
when I write to the parents of my students
I forget
where I come from

Maestra

Disculpa
que mi hija llega tarde todas las mañanas

Es que llego a las 5am
y trato de dormir un poco
antes de llevarla a la escuela

A veces no oigo el alarma
y ella me tiene que despertar
y es cuando llegamos tarde

Escojo este horario
para poder estar con ella cuando llega de la escuela
Pero a veces no sale
Ojalá me entiendas

In this week of parent conferences

I judge the no-show mothers
the way my no-show mother was judged

¡Huelga!

Mama, the last time you got a raise

was three years ago
and it was for 6%

before that was in 2007 for 10%
and now you are asking for another raise

If you do the math Mama
your pay never catches up with inflation and cost of living

Every year
you make less and less

Don't let the pigeon drive the fight alone for nuestra gente's rights!

So if the narrator of the Little Prince doesn't like grownups

and he's a grownup
how does he make friends?
And who is the Little Prince?

You will have to wait till Tuesday when we get to chapter 2

Does he ever go back to drawing?

Wait for Wednesday and chapter 3

And why does the illustration show a planet and a rose?

Wait till Thursday
er, I will be on strike on Thursday

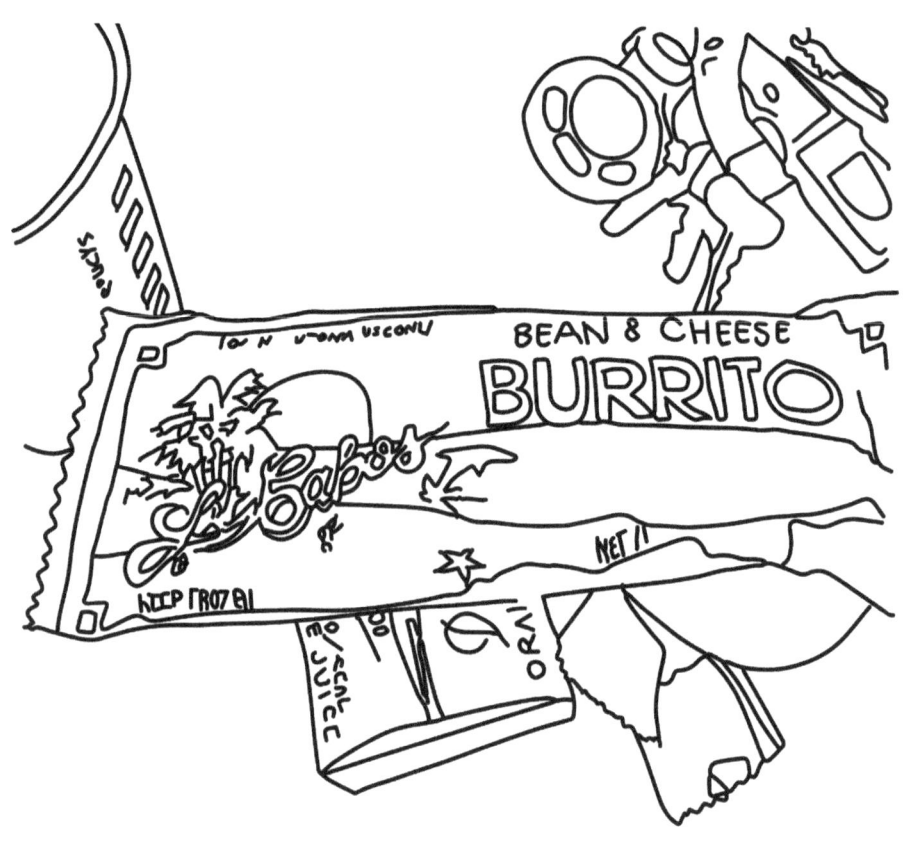

Omen, today will be a good day. 😃
#AllYouLAUSDBurritoHatersCanKissMyGrits

My homey's suggestions to supplement my income during the strike

1. You can sell weed to the teachers
2. You can sell water and drinks to the teachers
   like my homey used
   to do at the Lakers parades
3. You guys can start a strike fund
4. Puedes putear

Soaking wet from picketing in 10 hours of rain

Would Dolores Huerta have walked into her house
with two large Little Ceaser's pizzas for her children
requesting they sort themselves out for the evening
after they sorted themselves out for the day?

I kick off my muddy boots
Peel wet clothes off of my skin
Slip into lavender bath
Crawl into soft bed at 7 pm
to sleep until the next morning

      ¿Cómo lo hicieron las madres campesinas?

It was cold

It was wet
and parents
brought us coffee
donuts, tamales, pan dulce, tangerines
Costco wraps, parfaits, oatmeal
Porto's empanadas and devotion

They cooked pozole and chicken soup on a portable stove
under the oak tree

Their generosity and care
live in me

That time we went on strike and I discovered that all I am sure
about is that I love teachers. All those other involved parties can
go fuck themselves. Yay! 🎉

Since returning to work from the strike

elementary school teachers have seen no improvement
in our classroom life
and a deterioration of our home life
due to a monthly deduction for our strike days

No raise yet
No retro check
and no one seems to be talking about it
except us

COVID

8am, First Day of School

600,000 students
and 26,000 teachers
will log into zoom
in one hour

One of the most stressful teaching stretches in a long time. We are not prepared for distance learning at all. Total shitshow. However, thrilled that I get to see my students for 20 minute home room every morning. Everything else… meh. #TeachingInQuarantine

Operation

Ignore my children
Don't talk to me
Grilled cheese from Coco's
I don't have a student roster
Fuck your last-minute emails
that I'm supposed to forward
to families whose info I don't have

Three of us zooming in the house at the same time
I'm creating a contraband blog for parents
to subvert the district's iron curtain
of passwords and apps that no one can access

I look at the beginning of the year
like I'm supposed to look at the end of the year

I wish I was in my classroom
My head hurts
I'm angry

Thinking
I need
to

breathe

Kindergarten Zoom

Kevin
Kevin
Mute yourself
No
Turn off your mic
Where is your mom or dad
Ok
I'm putting you in the waiting room

     Mom calls on google phone

       Señora Sáenz, my son is in the waiting room

         That is correct
         You need to supervise him because he is turning his mic
         on and off, making faces and interrupting my lesson
         Let me know when you've done that and I'll admit him

I just had a zoom meeting

with a 19 year-old mother
who needed me to show her
how to upload assignments on Google classroom

She shared that her son
was in the high school daycare
and would now be
at the community college daycare because she is going to college

She apologized for any background noise during class time
and said that it's a full house
in a single apartment
with six family members

She said she wants to do good by her children
and she thanked me for being a kind and loving teacher

Crisis Teaching Chronicles 001

My naked lover is asleep in my bed
The gardener is blasting the leaf blower outside my window
Grandma who has custody of five grandkids
calls to say she can't get into device
Her 8th grade granddaughter
my former student
is on the phone with me setting it all up

Showtime with 5 year-olds
in 20 minutes

Today, my student got on zoom with his grandmother by his side

It's the 3rd grandchild of hers that I am teaching
The oldest is in 8th grade now
As we were doing student of the day
his sister joined next to him
Then another brother and then another sister
until there were 5 beautiful faces
filling his tiny screen

The most important thing about this home classroom is that I have a standing desk and I buit a fucking altar around it! Lmfao! This is my distance teaching corner. ¡Uf!

Chaotic information

about returning to the classroom
triggers invisible stress in my body
that I only become aware of
because I get sick

No complaints
Some of my homeys across the country
have been teaching in shutdown
risking their lives
because their psycho states did not allow schools to close
in the face of a global pandemic

Smiled through morning kindergarten zoom
Painted a canvas during virtual faculty meeting where my video was off
Want to lay in bed and not do my virtual evening teaching gig
But I show up like I always do
Care for two hours

Two minutes before session ends
Ayende is waiting for me to air fry tortilla chips
and paint the solar system

My student's mom joins the zoom
and thanks me profusely
for inspiring her daughter to study hard in Spanish
and tells me I've changed her daughter's life

Ayende is smiling as he listens
leaning against the kitchen counter

I have a few more hours of momming
and then I'm going to sleep

with whispers of me

      changing
                 a student's
                           life

First hour back on campus post-shutdown

Fuck you
beer truck
and neighbors
for double parking
on a school street
with your emergency lights on
while we're all zooming to school

God bless all the families who showed up
and didn't get the message that there is no school today

A spot for me in staff parking
Boom
Get to top of the stairs with all my bags
and gate is locked

No one is manning the entrance
I see a colleague pushing her son's stroller across the yard full of her bags
I scream

Dude, what is happening?

She says we have to go through the front today

I'm dressed for my siberian classroom
and walk a quarter mile, all the way to the front

I'm sweating from the spring summer sun
and there is a line
Folks can't find their QR code and are sent home

I see a friend in line

Sáenz, I brought you a sandwich
Wait, are we allowed to bring each other food?

Second Hour

A teacher peeks her head into my room

> Hey, do you know
> what the fuck we're supposed to be doing right now?

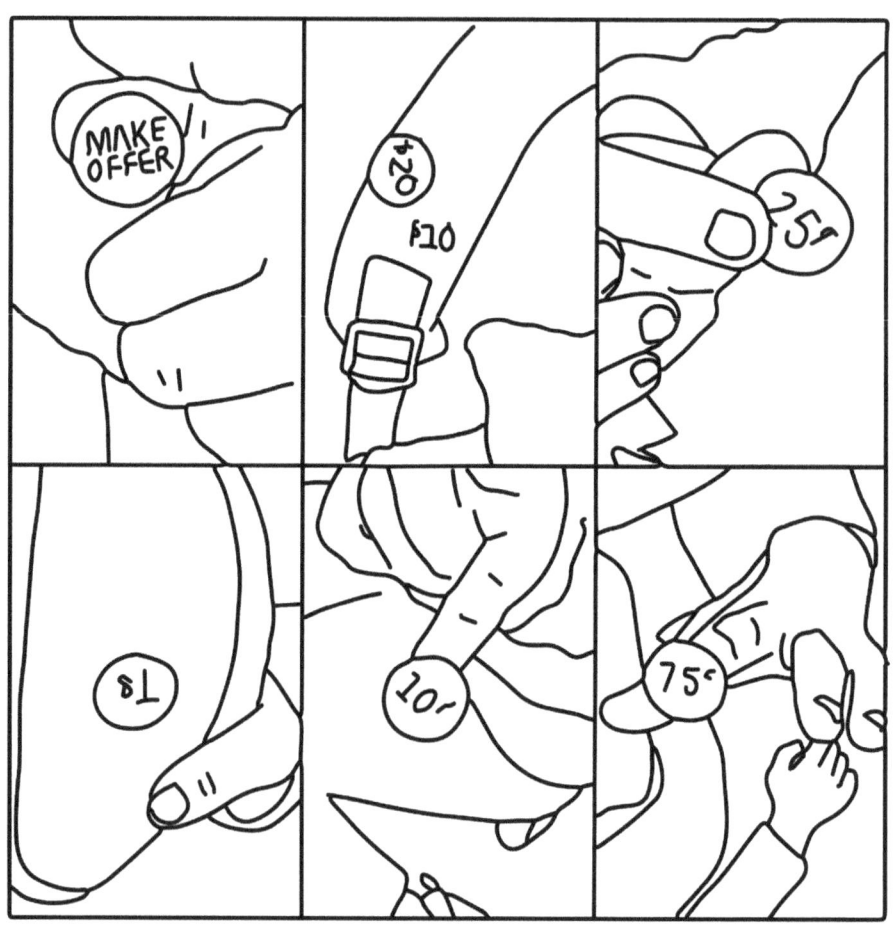

Students get this sticker every morning to show they passed their
daily health screening and are allowed on campus. I arrive at the
line and say, what's your going price today, kids? 🐌
#PandemicProtocols #FundraiserStickersWeFound

Brain dead

Look around my classroom
So much to pick up and put away
after teaching in person for three hours

Alas, another round of teaching on zoom in 40 minutes
and then I'll really be brain dead
So no picking up
now or later
I remember
the grandmother who used to volunteer for me
She would only come to clean and organize
Said that when she taught
she had a clerical TA and an instructional TA

      It's a shame, she'd say
      what they put teachers through these days

She couldn't get through this insane school COVID barricade
even if she wanted to
No witnesses allowed

My classroom is a shitshow
I'm exhausted
and I need to cover the mess with butcher paper before I leave
to protect from the disinfecting mist
they'll spray tonight

School district announced from one day to the next last March that we needed to pack our shit and go. This is where I stuffed everything. Setting up my classroom today. Emotional.

Policy

Instead of 12 hours

of training for teachers
to help us deal with the effects
of trauma from violence and poverty in our students' lives

Let's do 100 hours
of training for teachers
to help us organize
against the racist social systems and institutions
that drive that violence

I won't lie, I got really emotional saying goodbye...

Foster Homes

My students
disappear
from my classroom

Los Estiteres Niteres

Public School Ma(dness)ndates

I think
we're on candid camera

An experiment
in compliance and authority

The research question:

> When will grown-ass, educated professionals stand up and say
> this is all bullshit
> this is not good for children or teachers
> the institution is here for our sake
> we are not here for the institution's sake
> for data's sake
> and I cannot comply with your absurdity
> and inhumanity
> anymore

The experiment continues
the pile gets higher
the clock is ticking
and we allow
the circus to go on

My homies are visiting me.

**Children in my classroom are not allowed
to go on field trips**

without their parents' permission
Our school-day trek is closely monitored
by teachers and chaperones
Children accounted for and delivered promptly to parents at dismissal

Undocumented, unaccompanied minors
thousands of them
are being shuttled around the US
with no adult supervision for thousands of miles for months
Many die and / or disappear

I am with my kindergarteners for 6 hours a day

Most of them have been on this planet
for about 60 months

I am sensitive to the transition
from daycare, or home, or preschool
small class size, low student to teacher ratio, shorter days
and more self-directed activities
to suddenly being in kindergarten

To being in a room
where 70% of the room
is occupied by desks and chairs

This is where they spend
95% of their time

And during that 95%,
they are listening to me
working at their desk
following directions
probably daydreaming
trying to listen
doing their best
to learn how to hold a pencil
shape their letters between the lines
remember all there is to remember
about what to do with the book in their hands
or the paper in front of them
or the math story I just asked them to solve

They are earnest
defying their wild and curious nature
and being loyal to me and my teaching

They are doing their best to grow up
at five years old

But today
they weren't having it
I could not get them to settle down

So I said

      Alright, we're going out to play

We went down to the yard
Towering eucalyptus border the playground
Chaparral, arroyo hillside backdrop, soft Los Angeles January breeze
carried the monarchs that fluttered around us

The children were unleashed on the concrete pavement
Suddenly, they were puppies and kitties crawling on all fours
pretending to purr and cuddle
The boys became ninjas, wielding imaginary swords, jumping at each other
and crouching like tigers
The tether ball game
whose rules they don't know
was a gathering place for swinging the ball
and ten kids falling over each other to try and catch it

Two girls were telling a secret in the shade of the pepper tree
while a group of boys and girls were teasing each other and squealing
in that old-fashioned game of tag

Others were hiding from zombies
while a line of girls were calling out like sheep

to a few girls on the other side of the yard
and with some invisible cue
they all started to run
at the same time
in different directions
screaming from the top of their lungs

I don't disparage the mostly academic work
that I dedicate my life to everyday

I am a mother of children who attend public school
with the same curriculum and the same limited physical play
that makes up my own students' day

I am not interested in paying some inordinate amount of money
for my kids to spend most of their day playing
instead of doing academic work

I am interested in public policy that honors
children's need to play and imagine

But I'm honestly not working on that
So I'll just mind my own
public-school-teacher business

Sometimes, when I'm encouraging my students
to engage and pay attention
I tell them that home is where they can be wild,
and themselves, and do all of their shenanigans
School is where they need to collect themselves,
pull themselves together, and control themselves

But this afternoon
with the warm winter sun shining on us
and with our laughter and joy
riding on the wind

I couldn't help but think
that I'd like to say to them

    School is where you can be wild
    and be yourself
    and we welcome
    all of your shenanigans

                Let the children play
                Deja que los niñxs juegen

Color me not impressed

Trust me, a school's test scores
don't prove shit about how good that school is

but it does prove that racism and economic injustice
are alive and well in this country

Familia

When the principal took out
the wooden library catalogue drawer labeled S

in the attendance office at John Marshall High School
and pulled out a bundle
of forged absence notes
showing them to my mother
They both wanted to know
where the fuck I had been
those 50 days

They didn't believe me
when I told them
I was ditching in the Chicano and Black history section
of our high school library

They asked the librarian if I was there often
and she said

Come to think of it, yes

Shortly after
they changed the library pass format

I still didn't go to class

Ruben Dario
MARGARITA
Ilustraciones
Monika Doppert
Ed 10115 Ekacbunco del L

"Señora Sáenz, interested in any of these books I'm taking out of circulation?" I got a Rubén Dario poem/children's book and a first edition of Frederick.

Eating chalupa with my 2nd grade students in the cafeteria

A colleague runs in

Sáenz, the police have your brother at the entrance

Sprinting toward the office
I find my little brother in the hallway
hands up against the wall
and an officer trying to force him to go outside

Sin pensar
I run straight to them
like lighting, grab my little brother
(who was 20 at the time)
and begin to scream at the officers from the top of my lungs

My voice a lava rage
hoping to incinerate them

My principal, the office staff and other teachers come out
The officers said that my brother
fit the description of someone they were looking for
(aka bald and brown)
and since he was running into the school
they came after him

I told him that he was running into the school
to pick up paperwork to be a teacher assistant
because he wanted to catch the bus

that was turning around a stop ahead
and coming back in a few minutes
YOU FUCKING ASSHOLES!!!

I'm sobbing at this point
My brother is sitting in the office
My principal asks the police to leave

I can't get myself together
so they disperse my class and send me home
I ask someone to escort my brother and I to the car
because the police cars are still out front

We drive home crying
I sleep for the rest of the day

Shana Tova! I'm so honored the Haviv-Nelson family came today
to teach our students about Rosh Hashanah. We had apples and
honey, fresh baked challah bread and pomegranates. So special.
¡Mil gracias!

I'm in Vegas right now. I miss mom too. I'm going to have an Olde
English today, in her memory. My older brother's text to me this
morning. December 14, 2019

In my niece's Spanish class

their culminating activity
was to watch the movie
El Orfanato produced by Guillermo del Toro

My niece
having visited the beach and the house
where this movie was filmed
in Llanes, Asturias, Spain
was excited to see the movie with her class

      Did you tell them you visited the filming site mija?

          No tía, I didn't

   Why not?

          I didn't think they would believe I'd been to Spain

Amir becomes a teacher assistant at his elementary school

Mama
there is an autistic student that no one is kind to
I feel protective of him

Everyday I wonder if I am being too nice to the kids
Everyone is so mean to them

The kids want to know how old I am
They ask me if I am 40
I tell them I attended this school just a few years ago
and that my mom used to teach there
They ask me how long ago?
Was it in black and white then?

Ayende volunteers to tutor at an elementary school

Mama, I feel so bad for the boy I'm tutoring
He can't get up until he finishes his homework
And he never does his homework

      What grade is he in?

Kindergarten

      What is his homework?

Tracing

      How many pages?

Four

      I wouldn't want to be 5
      and trace four fucking pages of bullshit

I know

So I do a tracing race with him
And then he finishes
And goes to play

      That's called saving a brown boy's life, mijo

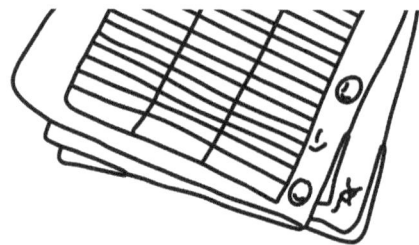

Francisco X. Alarcón ¡Presente!

To all the kids who are being told this week that they are not graduating from high school

I didn't graduate from high school either

My own mother was sick and dying
my entire senior year

I was catching the bus after school
to sit with her in her hospital room

Reward for being the daughter of a dying mother
banned from crossing the stage

I went on to live and travel
throughout Europe and Latin America

I have two Master's degrees

I say to you

      Shine on

Build your life another way
Discover and treasure
the true meaning and value
of what it is to be you

Reflections

**He leaves the warm dark morning of his home
and the scent of his newborn baby sister**

to come to this school
where he does not know the language or the people
and where he sits
for five minutes
with his breakfast burrito
unable to open it
and doesn't feel safe enough
to ask for help
in his mother's language

**Kindergarten and 1st grade teachers tell me
their students don't know shit**

and I think to myself

      How could they?

They've had less than two years of formal instruction
and often the instruction is in a language they don't know

My own sons
grew up with English
They had markers and paper since toddlerhood
to scribble, experiment with the alphabet and environmental print
They tossed around board books, memorized emergent readers
and we spent hours at the local library
When they got into preschool
they were ready to put it all together
and they have been straight A students since

Yet the babies who come into our classrooms
who didn't have the opportunities my sons had
are immediately assaulted
with our 1 minute timers and ultimatums
With our notes home to tell parents that they are failing
We put their names on charts for everyone
to see that they're below benchmark
The children who are learning English
in your English-only class don't even know
what the fuck you're saying, for whatever that's worth

Small children whose first literacy experience is our classroom
are expected to know and learn in a quarter of the time
what my sons had their entire early childhood to prepare for

I see a student of mine at Food for Less

It's only ten years later
and she's tall and beautiful
a composure I don't remember when she was in elementary school

She struggled those years
and we labeled her and judged her and referred her
and again I say
you can't tell
who someone is going to be
from who they are in elementary

Just praise and encourage them
Believe in their resilience
and human potential

Mi gente

Walking your child to school in PJs and pantuflas
I fucking love you

My colleagues think me and my high heels are ridiculous. I have
explained that they have replaced my red lipstick. 👄 This morning
I wanted to be comfy and wear estretchy pants to work and the diva
in me was like, "Oh no, honey. Fashion before comfort, girl. Órale."

The cafeteria ladies are trying to convince me of the necessity of an eyelid lift

What the fuck?
I've never heard or even thought of that shit
Then I was looking in the mirror right now
and saw my sun spots (that I'm getting more and more as I get older)
and remember all the fuckers who go through all these measures to get
rid of them

Pinche chemical peels, ni chemical peels
Pinche gente vanidosa
We're getting old, fuckers
Get over it
Stop spending so much money on looking like you did when you were 20

I never in my life noticed sagging eyelids

Until now

My career as a classroom teacher ended today. It hasn't hit me. I was hustling to pack it up and turn in the last paperwork. I drove away feeling bone-tired. Amir blasted "We Are The Champions" as we drove away and said, "That's it, mama. Good job." Happy Friday, homies. Nam myoho renge kyo.

#MamaToldMeOneDayThisWasGonnaHappen

My students are lucky my dead mama is not their teacher

Although sometimes
she makes an appearance
and shit gets done
in my classroom

I would like the term "line leader" to be eradicated from elementary school hallways

Walking the line quietly
facing forward
is not
leading

The minivan I am riding in on the
Petén highway in Guatemala

slows and a mother and daughter are pulled/jump in

This child reminds me of my kindergarten students
Jet black stringy hair
pulled back in neon green scrunchy
Shades of purple leopard polyester blouse
Jean miniskirt
and dirty grey diamond studded Cinderella pumps
She looks to be five-years-old

The minivan races and I look at her
and think of so many of my students' journey north

I imagine her arrival in my classroom from this jungle
and the psychological somersaults
she'll have to do
to make sense of a Los Angeles school experience

More than anything
I think she'll miss the side of the road
and the vendors
selling fried chicken and fresh fruit
and the cumbia blaring out of every available speaker
and the trees vines and branches swaying in the breeze
and her family
and her friends
and her freedom
as she knew it

Hey you, yeah you

are not
allowed
to be invisible
in my classroom

One day when I'm being interviewed about the book
I will one day publish about teaching

I will give a shout out
to our Tuesday faculty meetings
for guaranteeing me two hours of writing each week

#IWroteThisBookDuringTrashFacultyMeetings
#HappyFacultyMeetingTuesday
#WritingIsAllYoureGoodFor

Acknowledgments

I extend my heartfelt gratitude to Guy Bennett, who has remained a steadfast mentor and source of encouragement. His unwavering guidance propelled me to complete this manuscript, and his support in my writing journey is truly invaluable.

To the children, parents, and colleagues who have shared in the laughter, tears, learning, and love within the classroom over the past twenty-five years, I am profoundly thankful for your presence and partnership.

My gratitude extends to my sons, Amir and Ayende, and their father, Leo. They stood by my side as I forged my path in education, helping me year after year in setting up classrooms, moving classrooms, and attending evening and weekend school events. I am especially proud that I was my sons' kindergarten Spanish teacher. There is something special when your children attend the school where you teach.

A million thanks to the Corazón Collective: Carmen Calatayud, jo reyes-boitel, ire'ne lara silva, and Jen Yáñez-Alaniz. Your unwavering support has nurtured my creativity, kindled inspiration, and amplified my voice. I am deeply appreciative that we are regularly in each other's orbit.

In our third collaboration, I wish to express my gratitude to artist Lorna Alkana. Her love and dedication to illustrating the world according to Angelina is a gift to me.

Edward Vidaurre and FlowerSong Press remain instrumental as gate-openers for emerging writers of color like myself. You create so many possibilities.

Lastly, thank you to my mentor, Daisaku Ikeda. His teachings remind me that the essence of teaching lies in honoring and nurturing the humanity and dignity of each child in my care.

When this cabrona reaches out. ¡Ojo, planeta!

About the Author

Angelina Sáenz is an award-winning educator and poet whose work focuses on memory, mujeres and motherhood. She is a UCLA Writing Project fellow, an alumna of the VONA/Voices Workshop for Writers of Color and a Macondo Writer's Workshop Fellow. Her poetry has appeared in venues such as *Diálogo*, Split this Rock, Out of Anonymity, Angels Flight Literary West, Every Other, Cockpit Revue Paris and The Acentos Review. Her debut book of poetry *Edgecliff* was released in December of 2021 with FlowerSong Press. *Maestra* is her second poetry collection.

About the Illustrator

Lorna Alkana is an artist, writer, graphic designer, and teacher. Her interactive, glowing installations have been featured at music festivals (Music Tastes Good, Broke LA, Play Like a Girl) and cultural institutions throughout Southern California (LA Center for Digital Art, The Montalban, ReDiscover LA). Alkana studied Creative Writing at USC and Graphic Design at Otis. She teaches Writing to Art students at CSULB and writes autobiographical blurbs in third person. Find her arting on her process blog lornaphone.com.

In Praise of *Maestra*

Aplausos para (la) *Maestra*! En este salón de poemas, La Maestra Angelina Sáenz listens/writes with her heart wide open and a class consciousness that captures the many nuances of public school teaching. Taking center stage in Sáenz's collection are the too often unheard voices and stories of barrio children, parents, and educators. A kindergartner shows up to school with a broken thumb and an arm fractured by a steel door that closed on him while he was visiting his father in jail. Another child cries when sharing that their father was whisked away in a plane to El Salvador, "porque no tiene papeles."

Children in these poems are caregivers and alarm clocks for their parents who work the night shift. Children in these poems navigate so much they show up to school and quietly clutch burritos like lifelines. "Let the children play/ Deja que los niñxs juegen," Sáenz insists while pointing out major failures in public school policy and practices—from packed classrooms to oppressive testing and data collecting to pandemic Zoom teaching madness sans any real structural support.

Despite all the institutionalized shenanigans and huelgas in the rain that bring forth little to no change, La Maestra Sáenz is steadfast in her ability to see and love her students (so hard and so tenderly) in and beyond the classroom, reminding them in every poem, "Shine on/ Build your life another way/ Discover and treasure/ the true meaning and value/ of what it is to be you." A master at capturing layered moments in concise /compact language, Sáenz offers us poems that reveal everyday barrio verdades. The school is often a flawed and cold structure, but La Maestra in this collection is the expanding heart—en vivo y en poesía—of the children and gente she works with.

—**Olga García Echeverría**, author of
Falling Angels: Cuentos y Poemas

Angelina Sáenz's latest book of poems *Maestra* is equal parts indictment of the structural inequalities in schools that we allow to continue, a love letter to the children in her Echo Park classroom and their hard-working parents, and a call to arms—a challenge to open our hearts and our eyes to the gifts children bring to our classrooms and to our society—and to stand up for them. How fortunate we are that Señora Sáenz is still at it, nurturing and encouraging her children to bring their whole self to the classroom and the playground.

I had intended to pick just one of her poems to reflect on her place among our finest poets and writers—what a fool's errand. So, let me just say, nobody, not Clemens, Terkel, or any other American writer sets a scene like our poet laureate of the Barrio. Angelina is a rarity among poets, the embodiment of Con Safos, ready to light you up when you are just asking for a "tune up" and humble enough to tell on herself too. She generously shares a precious of gift—the honor of "seeing" the children in her classroom through her eyes and her heart, the heart of the Bodhisattva. Maestra should be required reading in every graduate school of education and public policy school in this country—and every school of theology too.

—**Rubén Lizardo**, Director, Local Government
and Community Relations, UC Berkely

Maestra Sáenz is a teacher, by career and by heart. Her poetry speaks to children who are strong, who are fragile, who are nervous, who are gutsy. Her words speak to what teachers, the good ones, see and do every day. She writes about children who struggle with new homes, with no homes, new languages, new faces in their lives. And she never gives up. Her own life has not been perfect and it has made her an empath for her students and their families, for. her colleagues and the ladies in the cafeteria. The poetry speaks to how hard it is to be that understanding teacher during Covid and close-downs and teacher strikes and with people who don't understand. The poems talk about making children feel valued and their parents understood. The poems will move you to tears. If they don't, they should.

—**Cheryl Ortega**, teacher for 53 years

Captivating and emotionally charged, this book truly tugs at your heartstrings while also delivering moments of laughter. Angelina masterfully captures the rollercoaster of experiences faced by both teachers and students, encompassing their physical, mental, and emotional joys and struggles. With its healing and empowering message, it's a must-read for anyone who has ever walked the path of a student and educator.

—**Rita Suh**, Ed.D., Lecturer
at California State University, Long Beach

Maestra is a meditation on 23 years of teaching in LAUSD at majority brown schools, where some students are in foster care, struggle to make it to class on time with graveyard-working parents and spend weekends visiting incarcerated parents. Señora Sáenz, as she was known in the classroom, was a legend at Aldama Elementary School in Highland Park, where she taught for 15 years and revolutionized the system with a successful Dual Language program she founded in 2008. The product of an alcoholic mother who was judged by teachers the way she caught herself doing to no-show parents during conferences, Sáenz writes with compassion, depth and realness that only a high school dropout-turned scholar who moonlights as a spoken word poet can. She paints the plight of teachers who strike during storms only to see no real change, deal with disease and displacement, and work for a system that doesn't pay them a living wage.

Sáenz is straight up and unorthodox, admitting she wrote the book during weekly faculty meetings, which perhaps helped her heal from teaching through the time of Covid as tech illiterate parents stood idly by and the world turned upside down. For anyone who has any doubt about why people go into the teaching profession, this book is for you. Crying in solidarity with a student who was absent because they were saying goodbye to a parent who's undocumented is not in the job description, but Sáenz is down for the task.

—**Kamren Curiel**, Writer and Mother

"Hey you, Yeah you are not allowed to be invisible in my classroom."

Within the pages of teacher Angelina Sáenz' book of poetry, *Maestra*, you immediately see what she sees every day, every year, for nearly twenty years.

You encounter snapshots of the innate brilliance, unyielding capacity to learn, and tender exchanges of love and care between a culturally competent teacher and her pupils. Between a distinguished educator and her school. And between a contemplative daughter, mother, and writer and her proximate loved ones and the larger world that surrounds all of us.

Simultaneously in gut-wrenching prose, *Maestra* also illustrates systemic affronts to the deserved dignity of those who fill her classrooms, work in her school community, and share her life.

We get a front row view to it all as Angelina reminds us that at its core, more than anything, education in the United States and across the globe is a profoundly human endeavor for all involved. An endeavor capable of capturing and cultivating human potential. Or squandering it.

Will the students, schools, and neighborhoods brought to our collective consciousness by *Maestra* get the requisite attention, equitable resources, and desired opportunity envisioned for all learners across our nation?

Only if daily education practice, local school systems, and civic leaders determine, like Angelina, that they will always be seen.

—**Val Cuevas**, education equity advocate,
policymaker, and funder

Angelina Sáenz's moving new collection of poetry paints a portrait of life aching to push through the barriers that circumscribe the lives of the marginalized. Sáenz takes me back to my own days in the K-8 classroom as a public-school art teacher. Her poems are songs that cry out for the humanity of disenfranchised students, families, and teachers; she tells the truth about stressors that routinely burn teachers out.

Her writing shows tenderness and respect for the cultures, experiences, and personhood of all her students. She is insightful about the detrimental effects that those teachers who are disconnected from their students can have on our collective present and future. The work is full of atmosphere, joy, and love, merged with a necessary bitter critique of oppressive social systems that we must challenge as conscious members of society. Sáenz reveals through this powerful collection pride in her people, family, and culture, sensitively describing her vital role as maestra at a public elementary school in Los Angeles before, during, and after the height of the COVID pandemic.

—**Glynnis Reed-Conway**, artist, educator, and co-editor of *BIPOC Alliances: Building Communities and Curricula* and author of *James Baldwin: Novelist and Critic*

FLOWERSONG
P R E S S

FlowerSong Press nurtures essential verse
from, about, and throughout the borderlands.
Literacy. Lyrical. Boundless.

Sign up for announcements about
new and upcoming titles at:

www.flowersongpress.com

www.ingramcontent.com/pod-product-compliance
Lightning Source LLC
Chambersburg PA
CBHW051206120626
46547CB00013B/1219